I0324680

LOFTY WHIMS OF GRACE

LOFTY WHIMS OF GRACE

An Arcane Journey

Anthology of Being
by
David DeWolf

Copyright © 2015 by David DeWolf

All rights reserved. This book or any portion thereof may not be reproduced or used in any manner whatsoever without the express written permission of the publisher except for the use of brief quotations in a book review.

Printed in the United States of America

First Printing, 2015

ISBN 978-0-9965119-7-1

Wolfmoon Publishing
Dewolfmoon@hotmail.com

All image acknowledgements are in the appendix.

Dedicated to
The Union of One

EMBODY

I am
Embodied
A perfect vessel
In which I love
Soaking impressions
Dovetailed in feeling
Expression stored
In pliancy
Ever vulnerable
Adaptive
Inventive
A plethora of genius
Within the skin
My autonomic savior
Exuberant sentience
Instincts palpable
In passion craves
Each cell thinking
On its own accord
To dress my soul
In magic being
Composing soma

WILD

Wild at last
Earth traveler inhales
Arms outstretched
Red sky golden
Basking the daystar
A luminary holding space
Empowering prominence
Rousing silhouettes
The flames ambition
Ever-growing enormity
Clawing the atmosphere
A halo beyond the ken
Hues drape the shadows
Rotation encircles
The spheres interact
Elegance mends
Dusk engulfs the violet
Daylight beds
The landscape sighs

FOOTHILL

Sweet scent of humidity
Dancing aloft, so bare
Enter the realm of being
Tickling particles of hair
Vapors floating into cream
Clouds waft as the sky
Drifting long told dreams
Swaying hordes, they go by
Scents turn liquid as they flee
Drops fall inspecting eyes
Forms massage lie bleeding
Not a care in the world to try
Entranced as a miraculous gift
Awaiting for you and I
Layers spring forth to gracefully lift
Awestruck, beatific high
Adding balance flows so swift
Recycled in rain, heavens cry
Laughter exudes when sometimes missed
Realize these powers, they spy

GREEN

Fertile base
Masterpiece of art
Visions paint
This stranded picture
Reality impossible to trace
First love longing
Wind throws a kiss
A keepsake of the abode
Regaining light to amaze
Leaves caress my lips
Sprouted limbs
Hang and hover
Tendrils of life
Breeze of motion fractures
Fissured source turns
Geometric maze unravels
Sacred texture
The divine mask

REMINISCENCE

As I stroll through the ferns
I remember
As I look to the wings
My heart surrenders
In this chord of ambience
My ear drums the sacred tone
Smoke eases into order
As I remember
The peak summons me
In the womb
She calls
Stones grasp, touching
A braided visualization
Soil mothers the alchemy
The rays of sun revere
In the fold of my lids
A vivid pool
I reminisce
My ancestor of one

VISCERAL

Oh this mystified existence
A tear upon my cheek
Lingering glance of myself
Forces primitive in me
Nourishing alive angles curving
Mother giving meaning back
My soul is quenched of doubt
Soft malleable radiance never leaves
Each day loses its repetition
Smoldering in the dusk of matter
Visceral life in the pebbles of the land
Look up and smile asking to make amends
Motion ceases and chance breaks free
Imagination sparks showing you through me
Altered unto being echoed in visions seeking
The dawn of my center returns to breathe

MOONLIGHT

Moonlit pasture
Statues grow
Shadow sculpture
Ether shows
Fog apparition
Twinkle gate
Stark texture
Burrow shakes
Crystal shimmer
Arcane flake
Feeble tapestry
Sensory drape
Liquid sheen
Transparent baste
Spectral frolic
Hypnotic maze
Weaving shroud
Starlit taste
Nocturnal visions
Illuminate

VAST

Ascending in the forest
Pondering amongst the trees
Lush frailty seeping through
Hung unto the clouds
Captured in virgin romance
Variety grown from blueness
As mountains arise
From vast plains
Fruiting towards truth
So easily missed
Feeling it upon the feet
Caressing the static
Rising from energy
Tumbling through canyons
As a speck in the sea

FLOW

Life as form
Reaching upward
Stretching gravity
Resurfacing outward
As the flow within a river
Always keeps each point
Forever new
Nothing is stagnant
Eternally unfolding
Unto itself

LADYBUG

Dreams nearby
Your invitation
Accepted
Protecting wishes
A dwelling made
Converging together
Signs you gave
Brought of faith
Resilience shown
Seasons pass
The days shorten
Snowflakes collect
In the corners
You're found
Dark night strikes
Adrift, calling out
Half shell walking
Your wings lift
Carried to the light
Cycles of death
Comes a baby
New life
A reminder
We've grown

MAPLE

Sweet merry maple
To see your spirit
A grand red orb
Or smaller of two
Dangling on the tips
An ornament in the dark
One year from last
Encountered as a child
So small and humble
Two cycles of leaves passed
Great size doubled
Reaching for the light
Now you look
Eyes cast down
Emitting wisdom
Painting of sand
Against your trunk
Left intention
To the wind of chance
Days pass
A new palette follows
Art of co-creation
Thank you for listening
A true friend

EARTH

Crystal caverns
First dimensional core
Power-plant beating
Quintessential valor
Transducing energy
Wellspring inlying
Obsidian cliffs
Turn stone
Currents pulse and bend
Pressure releasing
Flames become liquid
Gas gurgles
A pocket drops
Lifeblood of awe
Ceaseless geometry
Mantle encrusts
Canopy of branches birth
Mist hidden
Mountains giggle
Ridge peaks
Rivers boo
Movement illustrates
Canvas of earth
The elemental artist

WATER

Greetings water
On bended knee
I sing to you
Humble in honor
Soft silken ripples
Bathing emotions
Cover me as lotion
Skin sparkling anew
Tasting the nectar
Cells rejoice
Intonation hums
My songstress
Our duet settles
Strength builds
Power resounds
Wave's current race
With great regards
My sister
Primal feminine

FIRE

Bringer of light
Admired in heat
Shape-shifting darkness
Into the iris of me
Composition dissolves
Energizing air to be
Colors rise from the soil
To the ether you see
The fine line of power
Lava my heart sifting
Meteor carries your dose
Contrast interweaves images
Prisms diffract translucence
Extension from my skin
I offer attention
A gift of flowers
Mystical reverie

AIR

Sweet elixir of life
Respectful I breathe
Your supple smooch fills me
Aware, a present
I merge as you
My spirit is one
We are cradled in creation
Your rhythm slows
My organs renew
Carry me to lost aromas
A taste of the ancients
Wafting through time
Your perfect resemblance
Illusion wallows
Haunting the gaze
One to observe
Formless power of dignity
We are blessed to embrace

MOUNTAIN

Majestic spire
Air crawler
Devouring space
Weathering the vista
The altitude stretches
A peck to the sky
The past frozen
A mighty snapshot
Heavens inspired
Walkers attend your crown
Miles visited
Spanning the continents
Panorama opens
A further region
Feeds the hunger
An odyssey
Keen overhead

CLOUD

Mountains call the horizon
Molding pictures in the sky
Painting novel scenery
As the moment passes by
Fresh colors jump from nowhere
Clever moving new surprise
Fading through invention
Hearing thunder as faint cries
Puffs of cotton slide into ribbon
Each second gleams wonderful might
Just when you get these visions
Vast canyons have been sliced
Melting unfolds along trenches
Radiant illusions of this new life
Floating open blueness pinches
Glancing down back up its white
My being furthermore quenches
Whatever pondering just in spite
These gifts turn dark to drenches
Raining worldly glitter in our eyes
Earth rejoices, drinks then twitches
The clouds flirt and twirl by

HAWK

Brother hawk
Companion in flight
I journey with you
Riding the thermals
Vision so profound
Magnifying details
Above and on the ground
Thunderstruck
Feet scatter below
Some brave
Nip at our tail
Feathers as a blanket
I lie upon your back
Holding tight
Arms surround
Rivers edge calling
Stepping off
Towards the sand
Drawn in the woodline
The path pulls
On my shoulder
My guide follows
The teacher of spirit
Thy messenger
My soul listens

LIKABLE

Summer
Winter
Autumn
Fall
Sensing it
Truly
Pervades it all
Grasping names
Mind nurtures
Discovery
Veil of realization
Projecting meaning
Distinctions
A tangled net
Outward refuge
Of human impulse
Illustrious smile
Nature's likable disguise

CHANGE

Droplets of mist
Penetrate the surface
Of vast still waters
Illuminating
The underground
Across the forgiven
Fulfilled in the shadows
Delusional exit
Stuck in minutes
A motion
Missing the moment
Captive by false truth
Softly portrayed darkness
Slipping back and forth again
Life otherworldly
Decaying strata
Burnt to the core
Stuff is not you
It's a gift of change
Look under a rock
It's always there

UNDER

What it is
Where I wander
A quivering notion
I feel it under
What happened here
The day I'm born
Tears love from me
To you I mourn
Touch me gently
Life in this song
My soul needs peace
Where memories gone

HEIGHT

The higher you go
Brings a lower low
If you keep it high
It will interrupt the flow
Can't figure the hint
It eludes the real
Time lost and spent
What's the deal

SILENCE

Silence refuge sweeps
Peace dissipates into being
All pollution forgotten
Ceased memory of the present
Rescue me in the whistle of the birds
Meek faint cry of leaves in the wind
Rustling tiny feet in the brush
Patience withers thin as pain
Noise disgusts as directions proliferate
Let it eat its own heart to refrain
Desire wishes to charge, reacting
Tires towards anger and builds
Bring me back home
Natures call of silence

GHOST

Sly ghost of freedom
Sip of child's thumb
Saliva of subjugation
Uttering the footage
An umbilical masquerade
Exit twist captivates
Afterlife jumps the cord
The basin washed clean
New lessons embodied
Another source mounts up
Keys of human drama play
Music of the heartbeat
Joins in motion
The archaic grain

CONDITION

Such beauty beheld
The world upon our eyes
Ignorance can't reveal
Its airy nimble guise
Who is this persona
An ego claims it I
Culture ingrains the answers
A faulty boundary lies
Conditioned it's all a shame
Thoughts separate submit
Missing the same
Race around and mingle
Pouring judgement within blame
How can we expect
Learning in this game
Hurt and kill each other
Till were all forever slain
Transcending in expression
Gratitude for life
Masked in discretion
Eternity's forgotten spice
Struggling somatic depression
The troubles in our strife
Insanity leads the mission
The puppeteer casts the price

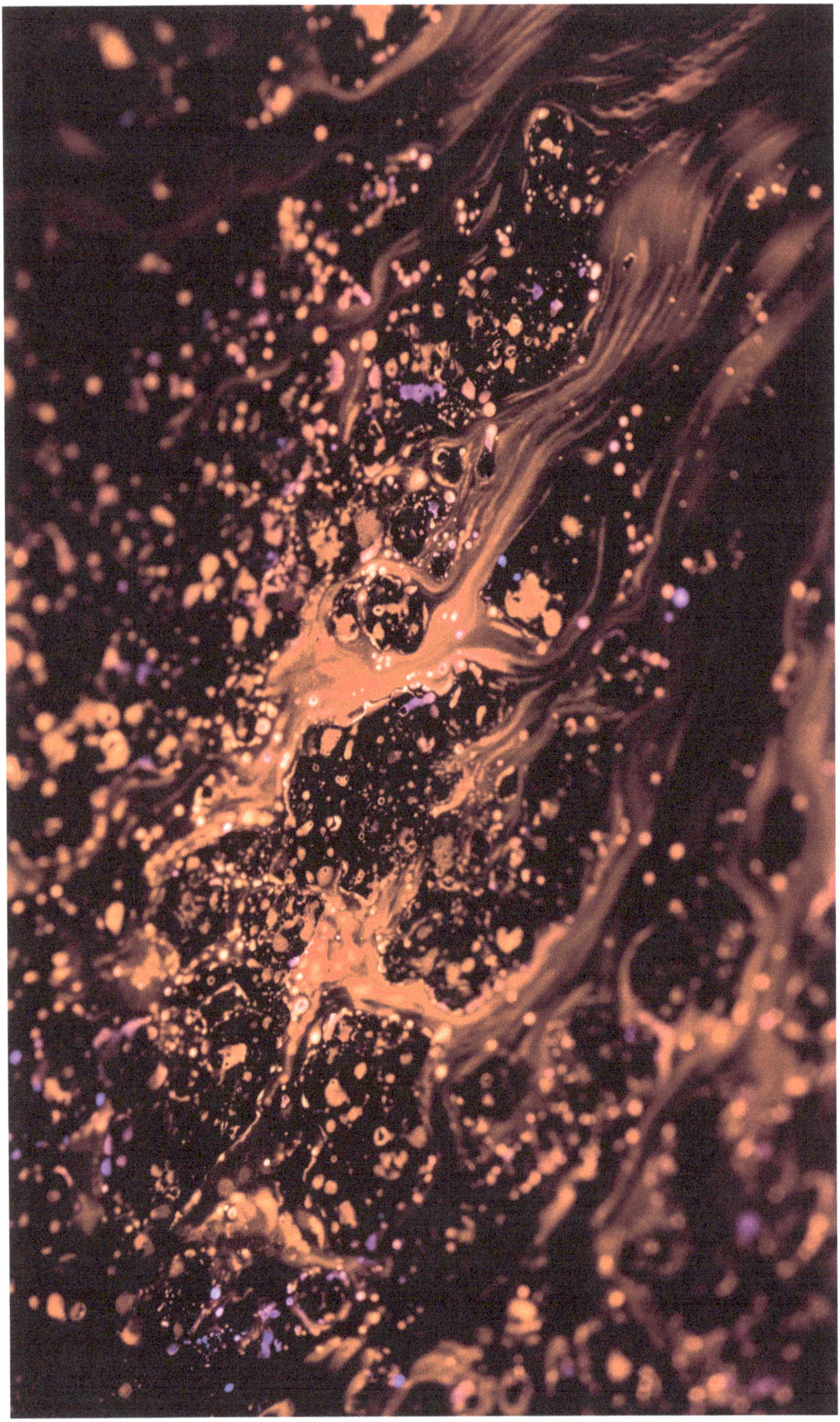

RETROGRADE

Dripping catastrophe
Patiently waiting to flow
In thorns of a drastic nexus
An impulse disposed as taken
Roving as human
Place to subject
Somnolent saga of man
Retrograde forthcoming
Lament of an epoch
The rift of asymmetry
Conveyed in unbridled denial
From designation of substance

HISTORY

Free delusion
Whose conclusion
Culture lure
Youth impure
History maze
Lies in phase
Money strain
Rich contain
Note paper bill
Elite fulfil
Danger race
Order states
Govern power
Human devour
Consummate slave
Early grave
Will takeover
Mind provoker
When it will end
The world can mend

CULTURE

Civil lies
Stay shunned
Property makers
Butchers of wood
Planet bound staker
Fed to rage
Overflow of death
Triggered cage
The cost of breath
Psyche as symbol
Entrails of unconsciousness
Tradition crumbles
Suit crows less

QUALITY

Alien in this world
Paradise massacred
For the masses
Fools flail to no end
Buried in petty affairs
Overwhelming desire
Clean the slate
A time to find
True friends
A small part it is
The quantity
Dissolved
But the quality
The thirst of quality

COBWEB

Shimmering memento of antiquity
Churning amongst the stars
Primordial spirit quivers
Purging regression left afar
Burdened ancient severance
The animus leaves its scar
Entwined it beams advancing
A shift of what we are
Mass forming vapor letting go
Aboriginal dreaming eye
Closed so long, a cobweb shows
Preserved in a lullaby
First glancing a repertoire
Novel images dashing by
Primeval hopes mix to belong
Human laughter yearns to cry

RECOLLECTION

Recall the beauty
Often left untold
Despite its troubles
Grief inside withholds
Deception hangs within it
Swept right in together
The secret never fades
It tests your evolution
Hiding it becomes the past
Somewhere you fear it's lost
To only find it in a tear
Washed as dust below
A barren home of life
Offering that speck of freedom
Escape to the curtain call
It's in the balance
If you could only keep the awe

ENVISION

Cycles of inseparability
Roam the depths of matter
Longing for new expression
In the crest of attention
Little known unfolding
Slightly forbidden
Locked within
True manipulation
Lying dormant
Every time forgotten
Never wilting
Engrained in purest form
Uniform that is
Repressed as the sum
In bewilderment of what's wrong
Answers here so long
Lurking out of phase
Struggling to set free
A knowledge flowing through
Mistaken to be me
Novelty came in you
Experiencing it is the key
Instances are arranging
A love beyond feeling
Sitting and becoming
Doing nothing
At ease

PICTURE

Place of meaning
Cosmic picture show
Browsing the planet
Sincerity amidst the frost
A blustery spirit afloat
The tide transfigures ice
A tether cycles
In promiscuity of rationale
Nemesis to liberty
Defiant in hearsay
Form to chaos
Shedding skin
Rebel of fear
Yields mastery

WANDER

Pray to the wanderers
Whether to or for
Received less fortune of others
A double sided door
The riches within
Success of the few
The wealth is
Closest for you
In the deepest dark
Shines a brighter light
Patience observing
The scene passes
A wave in the ocean
Breaking on the shore
Merges with its grandiosity
The source
From which it came

WORMHOLE

In the sorrow of thought
Weeping pain and pleasure
Suffering slows down
Come compassion gather
Solemn gracious humility
My bones enchant the hollows
Initiation chimes to enter
Endorphins flood
The optic looking glass
Holographic receptor is tuned
The black hole draws marrow
Tissues magnetize its pull
Into the wormhole I go

CHOICE

Fear waits in haste
A turnover of pain
The mind reels it in
Hooked in a loop
Feedback of what was
Observation calls
Awareness exhales
Stepping out
Unafraid
To love I choose
My lungs fill
Empowered is my heart
Full is the will
Authentic wisdom

BREATH

Sacred web of eyelids
Attuning the pool of mirrors
Underlying duality swarms
Cast me unknown crying
The whisper of ancestors
Entombed amongst my flesh
Hints spring out as dust
Innocence of life in air
My love originated who you are
A spore fossilized in mother
Twists crisp notes to listen
The smoke invades and sweats
Rescue me in the shaman's breath

ALTERED

Time slows
Air hovers
Fluidity arrives
Energy exposes
A cloud of light
Surrenders
All forms seen
Emanating fervor
Alive the rays settle
The woolgatherer summits
Colors devote change
Aura of life weaves
Strings of spirit
Guide the heart
Source smiles
Breathes of itself

SYNCHRONIZE

The world teaches
Indirectly it speaks
Seeds are sown
In the passing of flocks
Huddling of prey
Feeding the mammals breath
Feathers in flight
At fancy with meaning
Warming inside its felt
The wild talks
A hunch pokes your belly
As dreams uphold
Unconscious tickles
Tapping on your shoulder
A whisper to the ear
Synthesis of attraction
A coalesced synchronous event
Symbolic medicine

INVITATION

Curiosity floats free within the depths of my mind
Pure beauty revealed so gentle and kind
I listen content as you talk softly but clear
I wonder of the images that dance as I hear
A mystery flows through me
Concealed in sweet tranquility
Bringing tenderness of nature in still reality
The thought of you stirs compassion to cover my soul
A fragile touch my heart remembers
Infinity that fills me whole
Who knows what may come hidden in this unseen mist
The lure of events brings awe that trembles
My core seems to twist
I wish we might grow to know each other a lot more
Not just a dream to be discovered
Lying behind a future door
What lies beneath this picture
Can be nourished if you choose
My existence is saturated
With a flowering memory of you

CONJURING

Absence of thoughts
Enter elements within
Woven foreshadowed
Cascading to blend
Asking for admission
The light seeps in
Not what you may think
Quite twisted to you
Sustained arcana
Dominion waiting muse
Looking to pass over
Invoking the medium
Fusion ignites fruition
You may feel it
On the tip of your crown
Ready to blast off
Exploding towards the sun

MOMENTS

Always trying
To go somewhere
Never arriving
What happened to here
Not next
The moment is
Always fading
Where did it go
Somewhere in nowhere
The game of motion
Forever fresh
And free

SENSE

A sensation
Has no time
Has no space
Beyond words
Molds one in place
The solitary mind
Denoting beauty
Saying peace
Revelation as love
Ego hidden
For the soul to forget
The question is connection
To life that is missed
Chatter seems to cease
The sense resides

ETHEREAL

Ambient waves of ethereal projection
Casting vibration in a sea of consciousness
Melding upon the void of eternity
Existing as is, enrapture in pure bliss
Mysterious energy, undeniable certainty
Blossoming metamorphosis of that which is
Spectacle of imagination, identity transition
Beauteous moistened molecule of ecstasy

CONTRAST

Waking the tongue
One word ignites the other
Something unreal without nothing
Form unrisen unless empty
Light seeks an exit foretold in dark
It's all really nonsense upon making sense
It has to be, gibberish is the key
Amusing yes, it's all play
Just representations we can see
Hiding behind labels
Experience things as they are
Not who they are
There are no names without edges
Just presence
Running around
All these symbols
They close the gap
Who we really are
Perfect harmony
Open into all degrees
Pure infinity

DISCOURSE

Bound by expression
Lurking within
Artistic convolution
Whirling without spin
Belonging to be free
Turbulence severed strong
Sprawled out just to be
Words go on and on
Edified in this lesson
Risen from beyond
Classification for confession
Intensely prying wrong
Certainty eludes in language
Awaiting for the dawn
Proper communication
Evolving never gone
Conscious collective begets
Evoking fraternal bond
Rising from the graves
Of slightly tender lawn
Life's old clever maze
Hide and seek go on
There expression stays
Learning to belong
Marvelous cycles sway
The facade sings its song

PROJECTION

Seen in others
What you may not like
A mislaid lesson
If cared to try
Maybe a projection
Not you
But I
Ironic reflection
An apprehension
A message
If you like
Makes you think
What of me
Is you
Not I

MIRAGE

Virtuous phantasm
The safeguarded secret
Prophecy of matter
Invariably apparent
Enshrouded beguilement
Illusionary solidification
Emulating design
Portal to sincerity
Patterns departing
Reiterating uncertainty
Driven subliminally
Structured depths
Boundaries muddled
Manifesting space
Forget me not
Known directly
No blind faith
Experience for yourself
Come out of hiding
Dance, come in
Engage, let go
Alter into virtue
Welcome the joy

RESONATE

Noetic echoes
Ushering empathy
Sentient frequency
One amen
Distant chants
The wild blue yonder
Inland ardor
Fallen between the cracks
Waveforms resting
Extinction bares
Within the hours
Genuine alpha
Photons climb
Agape unto the gnosis

FACETS

Among unified incidents
Ruminations rest further
Healing the birthright
Bathed in the web of destiny
An atom of the quark
Reaching to the universe
Found in verse obscured
Dimension so precious
Such grandeur it hurts
Resplendent finesse

ENIGMA

Fall into matter
Why fall out
What is there, where
Will no end, to come about
Something in nothingness
What of this unspeakable
It wavers on the brink
A lampshade grounding out
Lair to enigma
Flicker of the brilliance
Passed the origin spout
Introspection suspends
The wonder exquisite
Foretoken of the known

OBSERVER

Time trap space
Thoughts of straight
Perpetually comes around
Nature blinded matter
Turn around, it's not there
Past, future misleading
Now is the timed endeavor
A spoof on you
Who are you
Arouse to hearken
Encapsulated membrane
Whispers all along
The fenceline is impermanent
Consider you are it all
Quietude is the threshold
Remain for a day
Obscurities unveil
Feel who transpires
Inside knowing self
Everything that is
Ever will be
Ensues the practice
Reality swells
Improves
Limitless
All seeing

ORIGINS

You are here
Original me
The seat in nature
Often I see
That wordless feeling
Objectively free
Laced in my being
Defying gravity
What you are
So true and easy
It seems your opus
Breeds spirit in all seen
You offer blessings
Gracious nativity
Delicate hints lie naked
Moreover wondering
Who can be
Your placid gaze
I notice reflecting
You provide unity
From beauty I please
Ticking the clock continues
From our blood to the sun
Who are you I ask
To give of me beloved

ALLEGORY

Daughter galaxy
Oracle of my sustenance
Great animation of spirit
A conscious source
Diverging you sacrifice yourself
An offer of inception
Sharing thus given
Incarnating light
The nameless holds space
Sacred textures fractalize
Esoteric spell of divinity
Assembles the call
The allegory of flesh and blood

ASTRAL

Astral cloak of desire
Take me wishfully
Night into day alike
Teach me what lies untold
In the valley of the desert
Open spaces glide forth
The little ones
Hide in the grey
The middle world
In transition
Just another option
One of many
A multifaceted kingdom
You may choose

LOFTY

Through the worlds
We appear discreet
As if through doors
We can live into your life
Bringing crystal clarity
Make peace
Through the grief
In the somber light
Miracles unto you
Are close if need be
Stay focused within
Light of the earth
Beauty brings
Treasures of guidance
You are lofty
In the whims of grace

CATALYST

Primal landscape
A candle of creativity
Catalyst of ancient memory
Pressure burst forth
Unable to contain
Fumbling astral sound waves
Mystified textures
Trance of conscience
The space between noted
Eavesdrops into the skeleton
The multiverse unravels
Sleep awakens taking flight
Coiled in the gossamer
The blueprint of an era
Impeccable stardust
A pinball in the cosmos
I join everything

WHOLE

One
As my essence
Penetrates the galaxies
Within as nature erodes
Always fresh novelty
Suspended in time
Bygone continuum
Where it all was
Regarding as is
Naturally occurring
It will be heard
As canyons without mountains
Would be absurd
The whole is contained
Within your part
Gazing afar
It is here
In you

INFINITE

Supreme infinity
Contemplation hides
In the crevice of starlight
Designing genuine intimacy
The wake of veracity
Playing the everlasting host
The fidelity of existence
Gathering allure unmatched
A bare core underlying
Committed within
Through realms muted
No longer restricting frequency
Entwined with pure potentiality
The candor is glimpsed
Realizing the inside out
The eloquent route
Evolution in presence
Assessing hypnotic acuity
Attachments fall by the wayside
A flux unending
Come whatever lost
It's all part of it
Inseparable eternity
Remembrance of the void

VIEW

How it can be
Endearing suspense
A fraction eclipsed
Briefly out to in
An amplification
Fluorescence bends
Follicles shiver
Conclusions send
Reverberating questions
Amusing to the end
The tangible marvels
A glow channels grin
Universe view in a speck
Prodigy raptures intuition
A morphogenesis

STILL

So still
Lucidity bearing fruit
Intricacy yawning
Harmonizing variance
Guardian of the expanse
Formless items
Cloaked in phase
Scents of faint measurement
Drifting, rearranging
Momentary lapse
The field creeps forward
Stretched through the spectrum
Encircled in fellowship
Motionless wonders
Of stillness

SPEECHLESS

You render me speechless
Gaze in part to whole
Swirl my being in circles
Reminiscing, eternity unfolds
Serving life as a portal
Symbiotic elation of my bones
Question of existence satisfies
Signified harmony known
Who to touch these depths
Immortality caressing truth
Spirit body mass mind slept
Gills in the soil fruit
Cloak of imagination lingers
Clairvoyant crystalline peruse
Love purified unconditional
Smeared in never-ending proof
The macrocosm peers micro
Infinity absolute

APPENDIX

IMAGE ATTRIBUTION

All images used are from www.flicker.com under creative commons licensing. I do not own the images and I take no credit for them. All attribution goes to the following individuals. Every image falls under one of three creative commons license categories defined as follows.

1. CC BY 2.0=Attribution. https://creativecommons.org/licenses/by/2.0/
2. CC BY-SA 2.0=Attribution-ShareAlike. https://creativecommons.org/licenses/by-sa/2.0/
3. CC BY-ND 2.0=Attribution-NoDerivs. https://creativecommons.org/licenses/by-nd/2.0/

All images under CC BY 2.0 and CC BY-SA 2.0 have only been modified with a smaller size except Front & Back cover which additionally has contrast and color change.

Front&Back Cover: "_MG_2244_5_6Enhancera" by Mark Byzewski, cc by 2.0.
Pg1. "Redwood path" by Grant Montgomery, cc by 2.0.
Pg2. "Antelope Canyon 054" by Allie Caulfield, cc by 2.0.
Pg4. "Sunset at Lakeview Park, Lorain" by Rona Proudfoot , cc by-sa 2.0.
Pg6. "Angels landing" by Kurt Thomas, cc by-sa 2.0
Pg8. "Rise and shine" by Kirt Edblom, cc by-sa 2.0.
Pg10. "Fall colors 2010-yellow aspen" by Coconino National Forest, cc by-sa 2.0.
Pg14. "Tree canyon moon" by Michael Brownlee, cc by-sa 2.0.
Pg16. "Glacier Point, Yosemite National Park" by Bruce Tuten , cc by 2.0.
Pg18. "Methuselah,White mountain CA" by Chao Yen, cc by-nd 2.0.
Pg20. "Hippodamia Septemmaculata" by Gilles San Martin, cc by-sa 2.0.
Pg22. "JOH_3393" by John, cc by-sa 2.0.
Pg24. "Devils Racetrack, Death Valley National Park, CA" by Chao Yen, cc by-nd 2.0.
Pg26. "Fairy falls" by Stokes rx, cc by-nd 2.0.
Pg28. "Another great sunset" by Tony Alter, cc by 2.0.
Pg32. "Temple in the distance" by Kurt Thomas, cc by-sa 2.0.
Pg34. "Photones works #5944" by Takuma Kimura, cc by-sa 2.0.
Pg36. "Red-tailed hawk" by Andrew C, cc by 2.0.
Pg38. "Kearsage, Bullfrog Lakes" by Kurt Thomas, cc by-sa 2.0.
Pg40. "Balanced rock" by Grant Montgomery, cc by 2.0.
Pg42. "Photones works #805" by Takuma Kimura, cc by-sa 2.0.
Pg44. "Jones Gap State Park" by Scott Oves, cc by 2.0.
Pg46. "Forest sunset" by Ryan Mcdonald, cc by 2.0.
Pg48. "Alpine,Arizona forest rd 403" by Ed Ouimette, cc by 2.0.
Pg50. "Solar eclipse 11/13/2012" by Nasa Goddard Space Flight Center, cc by 2.0.
Pg52. "Lava" by George Alexander Ishida Newman, cc by 2.0.
Pg54. "Snow, Like A LOT of Snow" by Zach Dischner, cc by 2.0.
Pg56. "Tree Butte Falls, Oregon" by Bureau of Land Management Oregon+Washington, Photo by Jen Sanborn/BLM Oregon, cc by-sa 2.0.
Pg58. "Hoodoo" by Wolfgang Staudt, cc by 2.0.
Pg60. "Huangshan" by Andrew Smith, cc by-sa 2.0.
Pg62. "Looking up" by John Fowler, cc by 2.0.
Pg70. "Purple coneflower center" by John Lodder, cc by 2.0.
Pg72. "Photones works #969" by Takuma Kimura, cc by-sa 2.0.
Pg74. "SaguaroNP_2015 01 17_0277" by Harvey Barrison, cc by-sa 2.0.
Pg76. "Yankee boy hdr3" by Sandy Horvath-Dori, cc by 2.0.
Pg78. "Eye" by Moyan Brenn, cc by 2.0.

Pg80. "Main lunar moth" by Carl Lender, cc by 2.0.
Pg82. "Blue lotus" by Yang Hai, cc by 2.0.
Pg84. "Mushrooms" by Magnus Hagdorn, cc by-sa 2.0.
Pg88. "Photones works #5377" by Takuma Kimura, cc by-sa 2.0.
Pg90. "The leaf" by Edmund Garman, cc by 2.0.
Pg92. "Photones works #3383" by Takuma Kimura, cc by-sa 2.0.
Pg94. "Sharp orange contrast" by Jim H, cc by-sa 2.0.
Pg98. "April sakura in Salem Oregon" by Edmund Garman, cc by 2.0.
Pg100. "Texture" by Magikphil, cc by 2.0.
Pg102. "The caterpillar" by Olivier Bacquet, cc by 2.0.
Pg104. "Sh14 texture" by Upupa4me, cc by-sa 2.0.
Pg106. "Sequoia in grant grove" by Upsilon Andromedae, cc by 2.0.
Pg108. "Inside stonehenge one more time" by Stokes rx, cc by-nd 2.0.
Pg110. "City of rocks by starlight" by John Fowler, cc by 2.0.
Pg112. "Dancing and swirling" by Emmanuel Milou, cc by-sa 2.0.
Pg114. "Double Arch and Milky Way" by John Fowler, cc by 2.0.
Pg116. "Galaxy triplet Arp274" by Hubble Heritage, cc by-sa 2.0, image not modified.
Pg118. "Nightsky" by Edmund Garman, cc by 2.0.
Pg120. "Infrared horsehead nebula" by Hubble Heritage, cc by-sa 2.0.
Pg122. "Eagle Nebula" by Steve Black, cc by-sa 2.0.
Pg124. "Milky way, Joshua Tree national park, CA" by Chao Yen, cc by-nd 2.0.

www.ingramcontent.com/pod-product-compliance
Lightning Source LLC
Chambersburg PA
CBHW050833010526
44110CB00054BA/2659
9780996511971